WordheART

THE POETRY OF HUGS

BY LISA KILLEEN

GWN Publishing

GhostWritersNetwork.com

DEDICATION

To my children, Lily and Brogan. My two favorite people in the whole world. Always keep learning, enjoy experiences, question things. Be true to yourself. I am proud of you. Remember the world is smaller than you think. Your happiness is all I ever wish for.

Be big, be brave, be happy (Triple B).

Forever young.

Love you more each day, Mum xx.

Do not wait for someone to turn on your inner light. turn it on yourself, it will shine that much brighter.

TABLE OF CONTENTS

Lisa Killeen writes of loss and love, life and death, and a deep existential yearning. The sense of manque is pervasive in her work, delivered in an unassuming and accessible form that will be familiar to many. The often formal structure, only barely conceals deeper metaphors to be interpreted by the reader. Curl up with a cup of coffee on a rainy afternoon and give this one a read.

~ Chris Jenkins, Author and Poet.

LOCAL SHOP

It started with a love of the outdoor world

Or was it the girls it attracted maybe?

A passion for all things fun in the sun

A local surf shop was born by the sea

A local boy with a heartfelt dream

That's how it usually begins

With a sweet little taste for all things fun

And an eye for the finer things

But it takes imagination, time, and strength to build a local
spot

Endless hours, sweat, and tears and give it all that you've got

St Pete is its home

Attracting folk near and far

Where everyone knows your name

A bit like the local bar

Over time it grew in style and flair

Becoming its own little man

With lovely girls and brand name gear

And always perfectly ran

It's come to be loved as the local surf shop

Stronger than most corporate highflyers

Maintaining its friendly "How do you do"

Offering the latest trends, appealing to all kinds of buyers

Surfboards, bikinis, trinkets, and toys

St Pete's little gem to discover

A surf shop built with love and pride

A true local spot like no other

Do the things in
life you love,
not the things
others want you
to love

Striving for perfection is an uneventful task

ART TO HEART

Tenderly touched by their hands
Their soul flows through
Gracing the canvas they choose for you

The reflection of feelings for your viewing pleasure
To hang close to your heart, to treasure

Let it speak to you
Offering words unsaid
A story to tell
A moment unread

For it is their way of speech through silent words
Leaving behind
A creation of pure thought only searching eyes can find

It's words from an open soul on canvas ringing true
A gift from the depth of their HeART to your heart

I'M JUST A LITTLE PERSON

I'm just a little person

I'm practically a nobody

I'm just a little person

I clock in and clock out

I'm just a little person

A small part of the game

I'm just a little person

I'm not sure they even know my name

I'm just a little person

A number, a name tag, a thumb print

I'm just a little person

A member of a family like you

I'm just a little person

Only here for a short time too

I'm just a little person

My skin is my home for my soul

I'm just a little person

My skin is what makes me whole

I'm just a little person

One of many in the human race

I'm just a little person

Don't judge me by the color of my face

I'm just a little person

Like everyone else on this earth

I'm not just a little person

I'm a person

Words are
not always necessary.
A person's eyes
will tell you the truth

MYSTERIES

It's all too easy to play the game

To take from each other, the passion of pain

Angers so easy, but love is the test

Aching heart of the mystery, above all the rest

Taking time to know each other

Trading soul to soul in the grief of unknown

Having times to remember and experiences to treasure

Taking pride in the body of pleasure

It's the missing part between the experience of living and
dying

The concluding part to a quality life

So, listen to your soul and show your feelings

And remember believe and never let go

Some born as part of each other

The complete souls that drift in the night

But all too many fight with the splendor of the bitter past

That's when the smile of temporary parting all too often lasts

Sad goodbyes and new beginnings

We are the chosen ones to fill the missing part

Keep hold of your dreams and follow the right path

Drift along the road of smiles, find the key to your heart

I highly recommend WordheART! This beautiful book will truly move you! The artwork that partners with the poetry is the added touch that allows you to see the beauty within the authors heart and soul!

~ Tiffany Willis, Executive Director with Rebekah's Angel

FLORIDA

Cherry blossom evenings glowing in the night

Silver-lined condos, the waterfront in sight

The sweet smell of laughter blowing in the air

The ripened taste of happiness, nothing can compare

Lazy days in swimwear, tanning on the beach

Blue seas and surfing waves, never out of reach

People playing volleyball, jumping to the sun

Ice cold drinks and tanning oil, the fun has just begun

Darkness creeps in so smoothly, the mystique of the night

The buzz of restaurants calling, colors dazzling bright

Lots of fun to be had, just waiting to be caught

Adrenaline swims so fast in every town and port

The night goes into morning - 24 hours a day

The world within a world, the only place to stay

Where dreams become reality, memories, clear and new

Come join the fun, make Florida a part of you

When you feel
you are failing
remember it
is merely a
steppingstone to
future success

SWEET DREAMS

I thought I heard a noise last night while lying in my bed
The sweetest voice you've ever heard, and this is what it said
Your life is yours to keep and, in each direction, you will learn
Sometimes you will feel all alone and won't know where to turn

I asked what should I do when I am feeling low
The voice said don't worry, your heart will show you where to go
I said it feels too hard sometimes when there are many decisions to make

Then it said I promise you when you are weak, I'll show you the road to take

I was troubled by such a promise, one so hard to keep
It heard my thoughts so clearly, saying shush my child and sleep
While drifting in and out of dreams I asked the voice his name
You know my name he said, you called so I came
Once more I was puzzled, no name had I said
He said, you did remember as you knelt against your bed

All of a sudden, a bright light commenced from the heavens above,
The lord had come to visit me and guide me with his love.

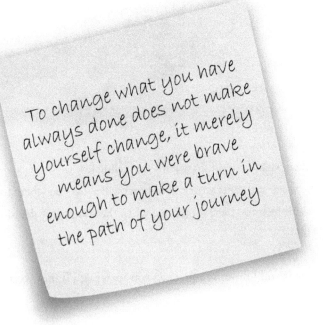

To change what you have always done does not make yourself change, it merely means you were brave enough to make a turn in the path of your journey

UNKNOWN SOLDIER

Drifting on a flash of light

Running with the dark of night

Fighting with the fear of love

Struggling with the mind above

Subconscious thoughts ring loud and clear

Mystery pain causing unnecessary fear

Desperate pleas to make it right

Concluding tears causing out of sight

Touch and smell in all you do

Too much future ahead of you

Colliding feelings crash down and mingle together

Like the mixing of clouds in the stormy weather

Dynamic feel of the wanted one

Burns deep in your heart like the glowing sun

Mad dash of feelings swimming around

Like a crowded market without a sound

Confusion rising, the boiling of blood

The sharp edge of evil cutting the smooth edge of good

Too tender to fight, too weak to run

On in the darkness the bright light will come

But when will the torment end deep inside?

Will a tandem keep turning or become a long, lonely ride?

The need buried deep down will keep you alive

Whatever the outcome, the memory of you will always survive

To dwell on
the past only
prevents you
from what is
silently waiting
for you to enjoy

Lisa's writings bring out the journey she has lived. Each piece causes you to reflect on your own heartaches and emotions. The suffering we all may face at one point in our lives. Her life of generosity and kindness is magnified in this collection of personal pieces of art.

~ Summer Schluchter, The Pineapple Project

HAPPINESS

A bright light commencing inside

The flow of the waves coming in with the tide

The glow of the sun warming your face

The magic of fresh flowers in an open space

The blowing cold breeze that rushes through your hair

Raindrops caressing your face, nothing to compare

So many simple pleasures, we so often do not see

Gifts of life that can't be bought, they are completely free

Enjoy happiness from the things the world can bring

Like birds flying in the sky and the songs they sing

Don't search too hard, it's all around

Just look deep in your heart, it's there to be found

IF ONLY

If there was a world I could choose, I would fill it with peace

No hatred or pain, all fighting would cease

No shootings or murders or fears from the dark

No more homeless people or tramps in the park

The sun would shine brighter when it came out to play

No more children abandoned and left all alone

All children would have parents and a warm friendly home

No starving people, plenty of food for us all

No difference between us, we all would stand tall

We would welcome our neighbors, ones near and far

Let happiness surround us and shine like a star

No language barriers between us, all secrets would unfold

And the skin color difference would be seen and all mold

The world would come together, united as one

Escaping bad feelings, like wild horses we'd run

Every bird would sing sweeter as they swiftly flew in the sky

And the grass would grow greener as time passed by

You were not dealt with
bad cards; you must
learn to play the game.
Occasionally
you may have to fold or
use the joker

YESTERDAY'S GONE

We live our lives clutching to memories of time passed by

Striving to do better and avoid living a lie

I remember as a child, oh how the sun did shine

But did it rain occasionally, and fade away with time?

The teenage years of carefree laughter and fun

But time is moving on and now there are goals to be won

Learn by your mistakes, live your life to the fullest, always
smile

A successful career ahead, but don't forget to have the
children in a little while

Life allows for all these things and more

Time gives you memories to treasure and adore

Life is precious to all, but unique are the memories we hold
within

Past thoughts of happiness and sadness that keeps life
continuing

Be thankful for the wisdom time allows us to gain

Through hard work, happiness, sorrow and pain

All of our yesterdays are gone, but the opportunities of the present are here

The future is slowly becoming the present, only to turn into yesterdays I fear

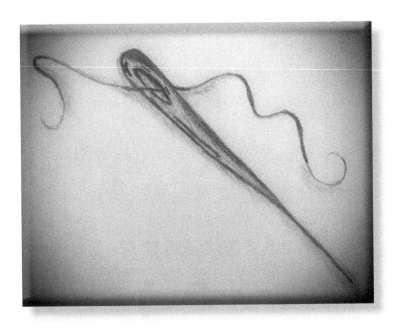

SILENT HEART

When a marriage

Is sewn together with true love

No matter how hard sometimes

You pull at the seam

The stitches will

Always remain

Intact

"I have known Lisa for many years, and she's a great soul. Like those of us who know her, you too will enjoy her dry humor, wit, and perspective. You WILL gain from this book. I did."

-~ James Chittenden, Founder, One Click Advisor

Negativity is an easy road to walk, positivity may require more of a sprint, but you will reach your destination much faster

MOTHER

You taught me all the rights and wrongs

In all kinds of different ways

The love and hardship of life to come

You prepared me through my youthful days

So many little things you taught

Things I will never forget

And although I still remember

Some I haven't quite mastered yet

There are many things you would change, you said

When you look back in the past

But all I see is you giving me something special

Quality memories which will always last

You taught me how to love and care

We shared the laughter and the tears

You showed me to have pride and strength

To help me through my older years

You gave me more than you'll ever know

A gift that can't be bought

I'll do my best to make you proud

And put into practice all I was taught

One last thing for me to say

I'd never want another

I'm glad God blessed me with your love

I'm proud you are my Mother

True kindness
is a gentle act
that comes when
you least expect it

WEDDING DAY

It started as a giggle

Then it seemed to explode

It drifted into deep belly

And then it began to off load

The room started to quiver

It became oh so contagious

We couldn't stop shaking

It went on for ages

We felt happier and happier

As it started to spread

The guy next to me

Couldn't stop shaking his head

The room came alive

Tensions all went away

With banter free flowing

Laughter bonded the day

Asking for help is not a weakness, it is a natural inner strength to obtaining a healthier life

"Lisa Killeen is a hidden gem in the literary world. Her poetic expressions of beauty and deep emotions, whether joy, humorous wit, melancholy, or sadness, are conveyed in a rhythmic style that is harmonious and eternal. A must read for those who wish to experience life through her eyes. You won't be disappointed."

~ David Nero - devoted fan

MY BONES ARE CHILL - MY HEART WEIGHS HEAVY

A passing thought runs through my mind
For the ones outside left behind
My heart weighs heavy my bones are cold
They are homeless people I am told

I hope your inner spirit keeps you warm
Until your eye arises at the breaking of dawn
And may your soul carry you through this extra chilly day
Sending you love and light, for this I pray

Be strong on your journey and keep hope in your mind
May the others that are more blessed always be kind

Remember you are one of us, we are always by your side
Together we can move forward, it doesn't have to be a long, lonely
ride

This chilly morning reminds us we are human together
We must help each other no matter the weather

WOOF WOOF

They come in all shapes and sizes

A variety of colors too

Yet there is only one special one in your eyes

And they are devoted to you

Most have big loving eyes

Tails that stand up in surprise

Ears can be pointed, floppy, or short

And to beg, sit and lay, some are taught

They may have long or short hair, silky or like fluff

Some are mix and match and others are pedigree stuff

They like juicy bones now and then

And are known as a best friend for men

They are so special in every way

Their simple love helps you through the hard days

So, give them a treat and say thank you

For loving me without saying a thing

I'm glad I found you, my baby, my furry friend, my
everything

There should be
a lot of love in
the world, not a
lot of things

TIMELESS

From the second I laid eyes on you

To the first few minutes we met

I have enjoyed our endless hours of speaking

And the exciting days having fun together

The weeks growing to know each other were precious

And they gladly matured through the months

Turning into wonderful years

I have always known from the beginning

That I will love you for eternity

If you are unsure exactly
who you want to
be or what you want to
do, this is truly fine,
however, make sure you
are 100% sure of
who you don't want to be
and don't want to do.

MY SWEET BUCKET OF JOY

My dear baby boy

How you bring me such joy

Your face surprises me

With every emotion you feel

As I stretch my arms around you

And you giggle with delight

I breathe a sigh of thankfulness

And hope to make it through the night

Because your face is waiting there to greet me

Bursting with warmth of a new day to come

Life I no longer take for granted

thankful that I am your mum

I only hope you can see the smile inside that you bring

The sight of your beautiful smile which causes my heart to
sing

To grow tall and strong is all that I hope for you

Holding on to your gentle charm and heartfelt humor to carry
you through

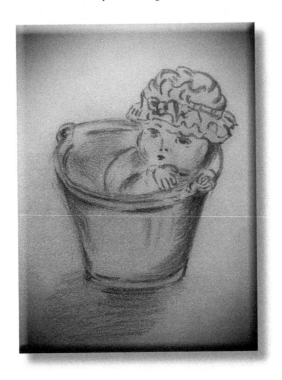

When I kiss your soft sweet cheek

I'm overwhelmed with content each time

For I will be eternally thankful

That you are a sweet child of mine

My dear baby boy

Thank you for such joy

SOUL CONNECTIONS

When the sky is dark

And the winds blow low

The rain does fall

And the loves no more

If it hurts to see

And the pain grows strong

All the sleep seems good

And all fun is wrong

Reach into your heart deep and you will find

The feeling of happiness of a different kind

The contentment of direction has left with the wind

And we are all born to confusion and doomed to be sinned

The body gives in to the feeling for trust

The heart lets go of the feeling of must

Joined souls we can feel for a moment or two

How long can I miss you before I love you

Starting is so hard like a chapter in a book

Will you read to the end or just take a brief look

When the heat is intense

And out of reach for the feel

Will the heart split in two

Or will the scar start to heal?

If I'm weak in my soul

Will you take me to hell

Or save me from sin or my soul you'll sell

If there is a chance to go back in time

Would our batteries run low or our souls sweetly rhyme

If I missed you forever

Would you call out my name

Would you run and surround me

Or seek me in vain

One chance that we get

Because life is so short

I'll think of you always

Much more than I thought

The most frightening thing in life I witness, is people living like they are going to get a do-over.

THANKSGIVING

Thoughts of past memories go through your mind on this
special day

Happy thoughts of things you wish to share and say

And all the while there are people not so blessed

Now is the time not to forget the rest

Kind words, polite gestures, are all you need

Smile kindly, be thoughtful, no more greed

Grateful for all you have and remember to share

In time, if these acts are continued, we will all learn to care

Very seldom, unfortunately, do we take time to consider
others

It's time to reflect and remember we are all sisters and brothers

Now go, enjoy, eat well and be blessed

Gather together, thank God, be kind but always be mindful of
the rest

You are only truly
showing weakness
when, subconsciously,
you know
you have the strength
and ability to do
what needs to be done

PASSING THOUGHTS

Imagine a field without any flowers

What does a day feel like without any hours

How would the sun feel without any heat

Can you use a swing without a seat

Can a face smile without any lips

What does a jigsaw feel like when the last piece won't fit

What use is a door without a knob

How do tears seem without a sob

Imagine your brain with no memories to see

Where would honey come from without a bee

Happiness is
a momentary
feeling, so is
misery - don't
prolong it

LITTLE THINGS

The soft lingering kiss on my cheek
The gentle rub of my hair to rock me to sleep
The warming texture of your tender kiss
These are the things I love and miss

The sweet smile as you say goodbye
The loving glow that shines from your eye
The funny face to make me grin
The comforting arms you wrapped me in

The sad look to make me weak
The sadder look my heart to keep
These are a few of the things that touch my heart
Making it hard to let go and part

"Lisa Killeen is a passionate woman with a heart for the underserved and sometimes forgotten community. Word heart is an inspiring collection of her personal expressions to humanity."

~ Lepena Reid, Life Coach

Let your dreams
take first place,
don't wait for
time to be the
winner

SMALL TALK

A whisper is spoken in the lowest tone

Anger strikes out like the king of the throne

Screams fight out in the highest pitch

A laugh is like a cackle of an old dying witch

A sigh of content is soft at the touch

A groaning noise we call a mumble is not very much

A cough is an illness or nerves it may be

But words that are spoken, are the magical key

It done so natural, just flowing from down deep

Vibration, then tremble softly, and out it does speak

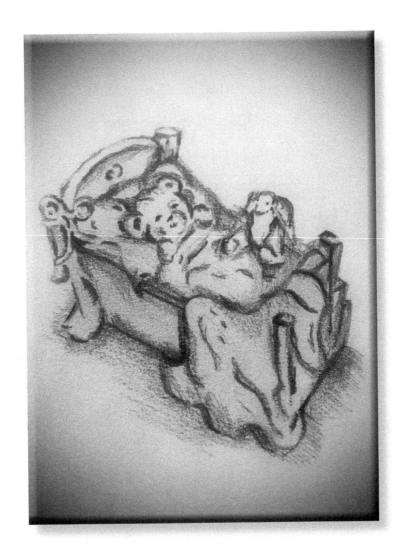

BABY GIRL

How I cherish your smile
All the while
You don't know this
How I see through your eyes
All full of surprise
You don't know this
How your laughter rings true
Giving me strength to pull through
You don't know this
How you burst with such fun
Like a warm winter sun
You don't know this
How your love you surrender
No payment to render
You don't know this
But the tempting smile of delight
As you wake to meet the morning light
You look at me and capture me in all your sweetness
My dear loving child, you are my completeness
I know you know this

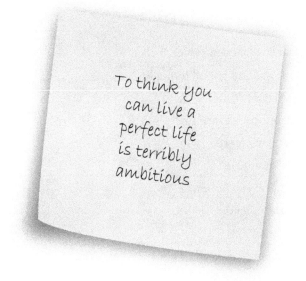

To think you
can live a
perfect life
is terribly
ambitious

IF I...

If I made a rainbow high in the sky
Would you go on searching for the gold, or just travel by

If I made the sun shine brighter everyday
Would you stay for a tan or go on your way

If I made a clown funnier than ever before
Would you laugh out loudly or just close the door

If I made the sea bluer, blue as could be
Would you swim in it always, or wave bye-bye to the sea

If I made the stars twinkle brightly at night
Would you watch out the window or turn out the light

If I made flowers smell sweeter, every single one around
Would you pick them to send or leave them on the ground

If I made food taste nicer than anything baked today
Would you gain weight or just waste away

But if I had turned around and never looked your way
Would you feel my absence and turn to come and stay

GARDEN OF LIFE

Open your eyes and you will see
That time is as long as you want it to be
Open the crimson curtain of love
And let the garden of sunlight shine from above

When days are dull by wear and tear
Look into the light and find wisdom there

The sunflower grows for strength to your heart
The petals of warm amber are your destiny part

The window holds the key to your smile
The scent of fresh air is the ultimate trail

So, when life feels like all seeds have been sown
And the gardens have shed leaves
And you are left all alone

Remember life is short and the key is to be strong
Pull back the curtains, let in the air

Let the garden grow and move on

Once in a while, along comes a book that genuinely touches you.
Lisa Killeen's debut is a heartwarming story with her personal
drawings and poems. It is an uplifting and big-hearted read. "A
warm hug in a book"...

- Elif Fitzgerald Founder/Owner PureLife Medspa

In times of
negativity,
rest assured,
someone else is
feeling positive
for you, the
universe is
balanced

IMAGINE

Imagine that there was no noise
And no bright colors to see
The world was lost in black and white
And the leaves had no tree

Imagine there were no mountains
And no hills you so love to climb
No animals in existence
And the day was without time

Imagine there were no feelings
And no one to touch or love
An empty river, no fish down stream
And no stars in the sky above

A world where life is just a word
The sea as dead as night
No good or bad, no sin filled things
No reason to put things right

A world without thought or conscious

No smiles from miles around

A decomposing nothing land

No soil upon the ground

Such thoughts are hard to comprehend

Too distant to be sane

The world in all its glory

Content to remain

TEMPTATION

Deep within, the soul creeps around
Surprising us with feelings, but no sound
Where will it go when it leaves the shell it's in
Voluminous body of the devil causes the soul to sin
No questions we ask, about the things we do
The acceptance of evil in every one of you
Swirling round and round in the silent thought
Deceit and deception in all that we are taught

The smile, the eyes, to tempt you near
The off given scent making everything clear
Welcoming the devil, it's the soul you sell
The temptation of evil leads to the long road to hell

If you smile
often it will
become part
of your daily
routine.

VALENTINE

Vicarious it must be
And then for sure it will be for eternity
Let's not wait, time is not forever
Experience the pleasure
Never give to receive
True in oneself, you must foresee
Invite, be scared, but abide
Never hold back, enjoy the ride
Experience true love by your side

*What a treasure Lisa Killeen's debut book of poems and drawings!
In a world full of clouds, it's wonderful to have a ray of sunshine
peeking through.*

~ Rain Butt, Founder, Gut Vibe Tribe

Misery may
like company,
but nobody
truly wants to
be its friend

WE ARE LIGHT

It is the strength within we grow

Tenderly nurturing the soul with peace and belief

Allows us to reflect from beneath

The body protects from the weathering day to its strife

Your true self covered so gentle

It's up to you to bring it to life

We are but an image of reality

Of how we believe it should be

But the glow from within is the power

And nurturing the source is the key

So, glow and be seen, your reflection is true

With strength, love, and belief you can show the true you

It's the love that we come from, the root of our core

The growing with time to show we are more

It's a continuous pattern, no end to how we grow

Water the roots of your soul and show them your glow

True happiness
can only be
found when you
realize where it
is hiding within you

I SEE YOUR YOUTH

I see your youth

Yet you are wise

I see the Christmas tree at 5 in your eyes

I see your first love shine through

When your eyes twinkle so true

I see happiness at the semi-circle corners of your lips

I see lines of hard work on your fingertips

I hear memories shaped in words of years passed

A smile, a touch of laughter, from your lips is cast

The knees don't bend so well anymore

Yet a dance step or two you manage across the floor

Tapping lightly to the rhythm of the beat

Music flowing as you gently stretch in your seat

Time is ticking and signs of age reflect, this is the truth

But through eyes and heart, I see your youth

Do not compare
yourself to
others or you
will never
reach your full
potential

FREE YOUR COLORS

Be honest and open and true to thine self
Life is but fleeting, love is the true wealth
Accept one another, look deep in your soul
Community tight, we can make it stay whole

Keep love flowing freely, always be there
Let nothing prevent you showing you care
If things seems impossible, don't run and hide
Vote for your freedom, shine with pride

Embrace your beauty both inside and out
Share your joy
Make others see what you are all about
Ask not why me, be strong and you'll see
True bonding will find you and set you free

Take chances but leave room in your heart to mend
Each person a token of love to send
Remember that love had no color in mind
When born out of love, we are one of mankind

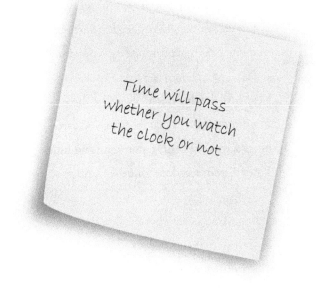

Time will pass
whether you watch
the clock or not

IN LOVING MEMORY OF

As we watch the sunrise break for a new day
We will remember you

As the blue skies burst with life
We will remember you

As the rush of life floats throughout the air
We will remember you

And as the sun goes down to prepare for a new day
We will light this candle to welcome in the night

And we will remember you always

Lisa Killeen's passion is contagious in "WordheART". This book takes the reader on a heartwarming journey using her own personal drawings & poems. This book is an easy and enjoyable read that can help enlighten, heal, and empower. Every coffee table needs a copy!

~ Lisa Lynn, Celebrity Fitness

You don't need
to try, you are
unique and
effortless

Guarded Heart

The angels play and find joy amongst the walls of suffering
It's where they learn, so they may do their hardest work.
Which is in the passing of LOVE...

LJK

ACKNOWLEDGMENTS

To my children -
Lily Fitzgerald, best daughter, and proofreader award
- thanks smart one
Brogan Killeen, best son, and dog sitter award
- thanks witty one

*Heartfelt and warm hugs to my dear friends that
have tolerated my endless questions and texting.*

To Chris Jenkins, the dearest of friends and a love therapist.

To John Collins, my fountain of knowledge.

To Lisa Lynn, the ultimate healthy power critic.

To Rain Butt, a woman of all things positive.

To James Chittenden, the diplomatic and sweet supporter.

To David Nero, my true No.1 fan.

To Summer Whitten Schluchter, for endless friendship.

To Kimmie, a pure believer.

To Paul Willies, the gentle voice of wisdom.

To Jonny Reno LaBudde, for always believing in me.

To Michael Kilgore, for true kindness.

To Mike Knapp, for trusting me with the gift of his fabulous talent.

To Tiffany Willis, a fellow heart believer.

To Elif Fitzgerald and Dr. G.J. Fitzgerald, for endless support and love.

To Jim DiMartino, for encouragement at its finest.

To Lepena Reid, a sister-helping believer.

To Colten Hollie, thanks for all the laughter, a true spirit.

To sweet Quinnie, a true gentleman.

To Lynda Taylor-Horgen for all that you are and all that you do.

Extra hugs for my children Lily and Brogan, Sisters, Sharon, Michele, Gail, and brother Selim, and an extra big hug for my Mum, for a touch of your strength and a heart full of love. I love you, is not enough words for you all.

From my heart to yours.

LISA KILLEEN

Author, Poet, Artist

Location VLVT Salon, Central Ave. St. Petersburg, FL

Lisa Killeen is a Florida-based healthcare worker by day, and a writer by night. She is the poet, author, artist behind the new poetry collection WordheART. With previous experience as a columnist for the Manx Independent, Lisa has transformed her writing on life as a local into a poetic inquiry into the human experience. Lisa has been a lifelong writer, ranging from studies of English Literature and several published anthologies, to writing stories for her children about fruits come to life. Besides writing, she spends her free time exploring St. Petersburg, watching the sun rise on the shore, and helping others wherever she can. With roots buried in Northern England and a soul residing in Florida, Lisa indulges on the love and troubles one can experience even while living in a sandy paradise.

CPSIA information can be obtained
at www.ICGtesting.com
Printed in the USA
LVHW010329160621
690357LV00009B/1548